REUSE, RECYCLE, & REAP REWARDS!

GARAGE, YARD, ESTATE, & FUNDRAISER SALE GUIDE

How To Get The Most Out Of Hosting & Shopping All Types of Sales

by Terry Scully

ISBN-10: 1495959031
ISBN-13: 978-1495959035

CONTENTS

ACKNOWLEDGMENTS

My deepest gratitude and appreciation goes to Sheila Groel, editor-in-chief-extraordinaire, for her continuous support, patience, and diligence in getting this book released. I also wish to express heartfelt thanks to my nephew, Greg Wright (www.gregwright.co), for applying his graphic design expertise to the cover design. Thanks also to Greg for recruiting our fabulous illustrator, D.W., whose creativity brought our cover to life. Lastly, I want to thank my family and friends for all of their contributions over the years to this project. I adore all of you--you helped make my dream a reality.

A NOTE FROM THE AUTHOR

Why have I prepared a sale guide, you may ask? Well, after nearly 30 years of hosting and shopping at garage, estate, and fundraiser sales, I've come to realize that people need and want guidance. Last year I encountered several sales where the sellers were obviously unprepared, overwhelmed, and, in a couple of cases, actually apologetic for the condition of their sales. I mentioned my idea to publish a guide that could be purchased to assist first-time-sale hosts, and the response was overwhelmingly, "I would have bought it!"

Sure, anyone can place items in their driveway, yard or garage, put up a sign or two, and people will stop by and purchase items. The level of success varies with this approach, but if you really want to make (or save) as much money possible, this guide will provide you with simple strategies and considerations to do so. Hosting a highly profitable sale is achieved by doing a GREAT job of preparation, organization, and presentation.

When it comes to shopping these types of sales, some people occasionally stop when they see a sale while driving by. Others are avid shoppers like me, those who seek them out every weekend. With the current state of the economy, more families are attempting to stretch every dollar. I have personally witnessed an increase in sale shoppers and for good reason. You can find nearly everything your families want or need at bargain-basement prices!

Whatever your reason for purchasing this guide, I hope you find its contents both personally and financially beneficial.

PART ONE: HOSTING
HOW TO GET THE MOST OUT OF HOSTING A GARAGE, YARD, ESTATE, OR FUNDRAISER SALE

1 WHAT TO SELL

Basically, you can sell just about anything as long as it is clean and in good working condition. Some types of items sell faster than others. Below is a general list of fast-selling and slower-selling items based on my experience. Of course, one key factor is how you price your items (more about pricing in the next section).

Fast selling items:

Electronics

Near-new furniture

Tools

Toys

In-style home deco items

Miscellaneous household items

DVDs, CDs, Video Games

Nearly new appliances

Baby Gear

Slower selling items:

Clothing

Exercise equipment

Old appliances (small or large)

Books

Out of date furniture, home decorations, and other household items

Holiday decorations

1: Does your garage look like this?

2 THINGS TO CONSIDER

I'll try to outline the "Things to Consider" chapter in chronological order, as some fact finding/decision-making WILL be necessary as you move from one topic to the next! Question: Why are you considering a sale? Answer: Get fast cash for your items in your basement, garage, or attic!

Multi-family sale

If you are hosting a multi-family sale, define what types of items you plan to sell and give people deadlines on delivering items for the sale. Once you gather your items all in one area, you will be able to determine how much space you will need for your sale. This includes the number of tables, totes, or clothing accommodations that will be required. Because you specify what you're going to sell and have set a deadline for others to deliver items, you avoid having to deal with unwanted items AND late arrivals. How many resources (i.e., people) do you need to help you? Here are some common types of sales:

Estate or downsizing sale

Moving sale

Neighborhood sale

Fundraiser (school, church, sports, etc.).

What is the purpose of your fundraiser? It is imperative that you determine the reason for the sale before you consider the next steps, as that will affect your decisions regarding location, resources, and strategies going forward.

Gather all of the items you will be selling and put them in one area (i.e., garage, basement, church hall, etc.).

Do not ever host a sale alone!! It is dangerous. Yes, a criminal could do you harm.

Have at least one helper – EXPECT CHAOS.

Rule of thumb: For every $200 of items you have for sale, have one helper. The exception to this rule would be a moving or estate sale where the bulk of your items are high dollar items such as furniture, appliances, etc.

What will you use to display your items?

Will you need tables, totes, Zip-loc bags, or clothes-hanging apparatus?

Do you have shelving, you are NOT selling available-to-display collectibles?

Are you planning on using driveway or lawn space to display your items?

Be sure to evaluate the inventory you've gathered for your sale and determine what you'll require in order to display your items. Do NOT put clothing on the ground in a pile or in bags of any sort. People will rarely spend much time digging through this. Instead, organize it in bins labeled with clothing type and sizes, or hang the clothing up.

Believe it or not, people shop with targeted purchases in mind ("I need to find a bedside table for my son's room."). By grouping similar items, sizes, etc., you will sell more of your items. For instance, collectibles, kitchen items, and such should be organized in a grouping.

Methods of Acceptable Payment

<u>Cash Only</u>

Be wary of large bills. It may be a good idea to post a sign that states, "No Bills Over $20". Unfortunately, some people use garage sales and similar venues to try and pass counterfeit bills in denominations of $50 or $100. Tell your customers that if they really want to purchase your items, they can go to a local bank or grocery store (where they validate bills of this size) and bring you back tangible funds for your items. You can stipulate that you will mark the items as sold and give the buyer one hour to return with the cash.

Hint: To verify those $20 bills, office supply stores sell counterfeit pens. Have one of these pens handy.

Checks with proof of identification and address

Be wary of personal checks. To really protect yourself, post a sign or advertise, "Cash Only". If you do elect to accept personal checks, ask for identification so you can ensure that the name on the check matches the name and address on the ID. Although this is precautionary, it won't guarantee that the person has funds in their account to cover the purchase. Accepting personal checks is still a risk unless, of course, you know the individual.

3 SEASONS AND THE WEATHER

Regions that experience dramatic seasonal changes are more limited in appealing Garage/Yard sale periods than those that are warm and arid year-round. Of course, even the nicest climates in the world can be impacted by Mother Nature. Note that avid garage-sale-ers will withstand the elements to get their bargain-hunting fix! Here are some tips on how to avoid impacts of the seasons or weather on your sale:

If space permits, have everything that cannot get wet displayed indoors. If you use your garage, arrange tables in such a manner that people can move around them while inside, but also so that you can easily move the tables outside should weather permit.

Advertise "Rain or Shine" if you intend to hold the sale regardless of weather. All your signage should be covered with clear tape or cling wrap to keep the printing on your signs from running.

GARAGE SALE!!!

Saturday, June 26 & Sunday, June 27, 8:00 A.M. – 2:00 P.M. 1999 Lucas Street, Scully Ca. 1112000 (off Holly Street & Crystal Ave). Baby girl and boy clothing 3mo – 12mo, baby gear, toys, furniture, camper, misc household & deco items RAIN OR SHINE!! Early Birds Eat The Worms ☺

2: Be clear and informative with your signs.

If it's cold outside, put space heaters in your garage and offer coffee and/or hot cocoa to your customers (they'll shop longer and be ready to buy as there will be fewer sales to attend).

LOCATION

Single, multi family, or estate sale:

Are you on a main street, rural, or buried in a sub-division?

Fundraiser:

Are you on a main street or is there an easily identifiable location or landmark? Regardless of your location, you can make sure you have a lot of traffic by having effective advertising and or signage (*see next section*).

DURATION OF YOUR SALE

Many people make the mistake of holding a Friday-through-Sunday sale, thinking that this will promote the most sales. This is completely untrue. The success of your sale is not dependent on the amount of time your sale is "OPEN". The success of your sale is based on the following four things:

A. Advertising or Signage

B. Presentation of your items

C. Pricing

D. Competition

(Refer to future sections in this guide for further detail on A-D.)

4 TYPES OF SALES

Single Family

Make sure you have "GREAT" signage. Plenty of quality and well presented items will draw a crowd. Add signs indicating that you are "Priced Competitively."

Estate

Advertise the types of items in the estate (i.e., "Antiques, Quality Items, Entire household", etc). Also make sure your items are organized in groupings, such as furniture, kitchen, linens, books, home decor.

Community

Many communities have realtor firms which are prominent in the area. Often they are more than willing to sponsor community sales. These are very successful. You get realtor-funded advertising and maps for your community sale. Of course, the realtor firms benefit as well by having increased traffic through the community where they have properties for sale. If you don't want to go the realtor-sponsored route, speak to your neighbors, choose dates and times, and post signs (a month in advance) throughout your neighborhood that communicate this information to your entire community.

Fundraiser

Gather your forces! One of the best aspects of having a fundraiser is the number of people who share your passion. Put them all to work! Whether children or adults are participating, if they all are spreading the word on donations required, or news of the sale itself, your profitability will increase. Don't be shy. Everyone feels rewarded when they can donate items, time, or can contribute to the success of a fundraiser.

ADVERTISING IS SO IMPORTANT

If hosting a Community, Estate or Fundraiser sale, I highly recommend advertising in both your local paper and on local free Internet advertising sites. The Denver newspaper, for example, runs weekend pages with the listing of community-type sales by location. These sites have numbers assigned to each sale, and on the adjacent page they have a map of the area and the number of each associated sale located on the map.

Avid sale patrons will reference this information when mapping their sale journey for the weekend (*please see Part 2 of this guide: "How To Shop Garage and Yard Sales"*). In addition, you should post your sale on free Internet advertising sites in your area, such as Craig's list (www.craigslist.org). Be sure to read posting rules and regulations for the site and comply accordingly.

If you're having a Single Family sale and you have A LOT of items, (more than $500 in expected sales) go ahead and put an ad in your local newspaper. If not, invest your time in making and posting good signage and advertising on free Internet advertising sites.

Obtaining A Permit

Be sure to check with your city or county clerk's office to determine if you need a permit for your sale. If a permit is required, you may need to pay sales tax on your proceeds.

Signage

When checking with your local city or county officials about license requirements, be sure to ask about restrictions on where you are allowed to place your signs. Some areas actually have city or county code enforcement employees who drive around on weekends. They will remove sale signs from stop signs, street signs or any city or county-owned post or pole.

Use store-bought sale signs or fluorescent poster board for making your signs. These produce the most effective and attention-grabbing effect.

3: Easy-peesy, store-bought signs are made to catch the eye.

Make sure your address and sale information is in large print so buyers can see it as they are driving by.

Some people place their "Garage Sale" signs on their vehicles, then park them en route to the sale. Always make sure you park in a "parking-allowed" zone.

If you are located deep in a subdivision or in a rural area, strategically place arrows between each of your signs to make sure people know they're headed in the right direction. I cannot express strongly enough the importance of strategically placed signs that will lead buyers to your sale! More than once I've wasted time driving around and never finding the sale. It is very frustrating, and most people will not waste time driving around trying to find your sale.

5 HOW TO PREPARE

If you really want to get the most money possible for your items, preparation is third in importance, after advertising and signage. You want to get people to your sale and, once there, you want them to BUY! The following tips WILL make you money!

Single Family, Estate or Community Sale:

Sort through EVERY area of your home, garage, or storage area. Look for unwanted or unused items.

Place all of your found items in one area. You will be surprised how much you have to sell if you take the time to do this. RULE OF THUMB: if you haven't used the item in two years, sell it!

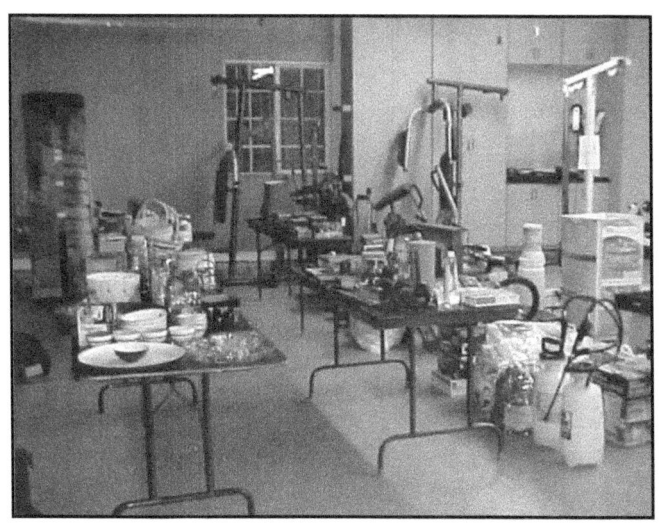

4: Doesn't this garage look better now?

Multi-Family or Fund-Raiser

As previously mentioned, determine what types of items you want to sell. Make sure everybody knows where to bring items. Set a deadline for items to be dropped off. Make sure you have plenty of resources, i.e., helpers, for setup.

PRICE ALL OF YOUR ITEMS!

You can buy blank or even specific "garage sale" stickers that have pre-printed prices on them. Price your items during preparation, not on the day of the sale. If you have advertised well, people will be parked in front of your house just waiting for the sale to begin. If you haven't pre-priced your items, you will be overwhelmed trying to get everything set up, while people are simultaneously asking how much you want for each of your items. Also, a lot of people don't like to ask how much you want for your items and they will leave your sale empty-handed.

Furniture

Inspect furniture for wear, structural soundness, and breakage. If upholstery is worn, determine the extent of the wear, e.g., is the wear something that could be masked with a slipcover or be re-upholstered? Is the piece structurally sound? If so, it is sellable. If not, put it in the pile for Goodwill or for the dump yard.

Is there dirty or stained fabric on furniture? Take the time to try to clean it. Over-the-counter upholstery/carpet cleaners have come a long way! All it takes is a few dollars for the cleaner and a little elbow grease to achieve a sale and profit.

Scratched wood furniture often can be made beautiful. Try a simple cleanup by applying a product called "Scratch Cover". It is available in liquid form at most department stores or supermarkets, or you can order "Scratch Cover" pens through furniture stores or online. By taking the time to clean and polish, you frequently can sell items that you thought were unsellable, even making 50-75% more on the sale of that item!

Electronics

In order to get a top dollar sale, make sure the electronic item is in working order and that you can demonstrate its functionality. Otherwise buyers will consider it too much of a risk and will pay minimally, if anything. If the item requires batteries, place cheap batteries in it to make it functional.

If it's electric, have an outlet available to demonstrate functionality.

Make sure your items are clean! A layer of dust, dirt or grime will deter buyers.

If you are knowingly selling non-functional electronics, label them as such and price inexpensively.

Be prepared for RETURNS!!! If you sell something as functional and it doesn't work, people will return the items and ask for their money back.

Tools & Hardware

Consider the age, appearance, and quality of what you are selling. Tool shoppers usually know what they're looking for and looking at. If you have brand-name power tools, take a few minutes to clean them up and keep any relevant tool cases, manuals, and attachments together with the tools.

Hand tools need to be clean, undamaged, and in working

condition. If they aren't, don't bother putting them out for sale.

Hardware (nails, bolts, etc.) should be packaged to sell. If the items are not in their original packaging, place them in Ziploc bags or some type of appropriately sized container. If selling hardware in bulk (i.e., 10 for $1), have Ziploc baggies or small paper bags available nearby for buyers to use.

Decorative Items

Inspect items for chips, scratches and other damage. Also check the underside of knick knacks for markings! Those markings can be identifiers for collector or high-dollar items, so check them out and do your homework. I once bought a gold deco vase for 25 cents and when I got home, I turned it over and discovered a marking on the bottom of it that said "22 KT gold". It had been dipped in 22 carat gold and was worth much more than the 25 cents I paid for it!!!.

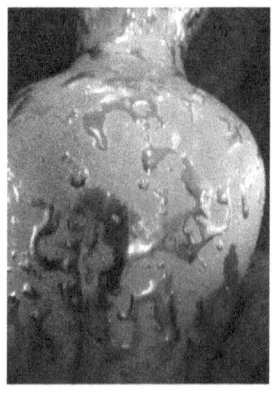

6: One of my favorite finds!

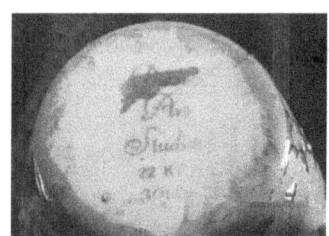

5: Doesn't that just bring a tear to the eye?

7: Present plates like this to minimize handling .

If the item is broken, trash it. DO NOT try to glue it or sell it broken. Items like this will make your sale appear second-class.

Wall Decorations

If the item has a wooden frame, polish the frame. Always make sure your items are clean! If the frame has broken glass, remove the glass and sell only the art inside the frame. A piece of glass is very cheap, so a serious buyer will still buy the art and buy a nice piece of glass for it at a local craft store.

Draperies, Pillows, and Linens

Make sure they are clean with no tears or stains.

Clothing

Only sell clothing in good condition. Do not try to sell clothing with broken zippers, missing buttons, tears or stains.

Toys

Toys always sell quickly at sales. I think this is because children enjoy variety and most people don't want to pay full prices at stores if they can avoid it! Clean all toys with Clorox wipes or Lysol. If toys are battery-operated, install cheap batteries and make sure they work!!! If they don't, remove the batteries and throw them away. Trademark signs on the toys are always a good selling feature.

Bicycles

If selling bicycles, put air in the tires.

6 HOW TO PRICE

Pricing is so important that I've devoted a special chapter to this. After having gone to all the trouble in the previous chapters, you want to make the most money for those efforts.

Pricing items too high typically results in low sales. People attend private sales looking for a bargain or even *the* bargain. A general rule of thumb is that you should price items at 10 cents-on-the-dollar of what you paid for an item (e.g., a pair of $20 jeans should be priced at $2, a DVD player you bought for $50 should be priced at $5).

One exception: Furniture or large appliances

If a sofa or a refrigerator is in EXCELLENT condition, you can ask for 25-cents-on-the-dollar of the original sales price (e.g., if you paid $500 for it, price it at $125). Be ready for people to counteroffer your prices! One of the thrills of shopping sales is to GET A BARGAIN, and most seasoned sales customer will do so enthusiastically. Don't be offended if you're asking $10 for an item and someone offers you $5. Instead, meet them halfway with $7.50.

Another consideration would be to examine the list of fast-selling items vs. slower-selling items I've provided in Part One. You may be able to begin the sale by pricing the desirable items a little higher, knowing people will try to bargain with you. If there are expensive items for which you paid a considerable amount and you believe you can get a higher price on eBay, Craigslist, or elsewhere, price them for what you want to get out of them and label the price as FIRM.

If you have items and you are unsure of their value, eBay (www.ebay.com) is a great resource to use. Go to the web site and type in the description of your item. It will come back with listings of like items for sale. On the lower left hand side, select "Completed Listings". This will give you the prices that items actually sold for. You can print the screen and place a copy of it with the item you put in your garage sale as evidence of what the item has sold for on eBay. You should typically price your item a little lower so that buyers know they are getting a good deal!

7 SETUP

Most importantly, always consider the season of your sale and watch the hourly weather forecast. If there is a chance of showers, wind, hurricanes, etc., plan your setup in anticipation of these conditions.

8: Outdoor sample presentation

Having a yard sale with no garage or structural covering?

Have tarps handy to cover your tables and all exposed items.

Place all clothing in totes that can be covered with a lid.

If it gets windy, place items on their side and cover with a tarp.

Take all breakables inside until the weather dissipates.

9: Clearly mark what is for sale outside.

General tips for indoor sales

Hang tarps or sheets on walls in order to cover any items that are not for sale.

If you don't want to cover walls with tarps, put signs up that state that the items on walls are NOT FOR SALE.

Be sure that people helping you host the sale know what ISN'T for sale! Even so, people may still try to pull items off your walls and attempt to buy what you didn't intend to sell.

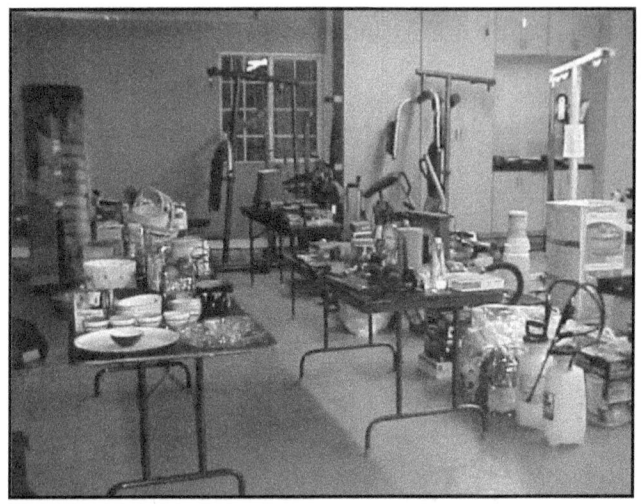

10: Example of table placement.

Place tables along the walls with enough room for people to walk on either side of the tables.

If you expect winds or rain, place linens and clothing closest to the nearest interior wall.

Display clothing items on hangers whenever possible, and arrange by gender (i.e., Men's, Women's, Children's) and by size (i.e., SZ: S, M, L; SZ 6, 10, 14). If you have no way to hang clothing, use totes and label the front of the totes with the proper gender and size.

**11: Large, easy-to-read labels
for clothing.**

Arrange items by category:

Place all kitchen items together, all electronics together, etc.

Place toys AWAY from breakable items and AWAY from the road. In case a child wants to try out a bicycle, he shouldn't be able to ride out into the street easily.

Avoid placing items under tables because people won't notice them there.

Display jewelry and valuables on the table where you are managing the sale. This will reduce the opportunity for theft.

Try to place all furniture together and, if space permits, organize them in an arrangement (look at furniture store displays). For instance, place a couch together with a chair and end tables so buyers can see how they would all look together. You might be able to sell a grouping of furniture for more money than if you tried selling them as individual pieces!

Set up as much as you can inside your garage the night before or some days preceding your sale. Items you plan to place outside should be staged closest to your garage door, so as that as soon as you open the door for the sale they can rapidly be moved outside.

8 HOLDING A SALE

Never host a sale alone unless it is a community sale and your neighbors are participating in it. Believe it or not, there have been incidents of robberies which are more likely to occur if you're alone.

Be prepared for early birds! People will wait in their cars, ready to dash up to your sale as soon as your garage door opens.

If you have small children, it is best to arrange a play date for them or have a sitter come in for the first few hours of a sale. It is difficult to keep an eye on or care for your children while dealing with your customers. In addition, if you're selling your children's discarded or outgrown toys, they may throw a fit if someone buys them and tries to leave the sale with the items!

Wear comfortable and weather-appropriate clothes and shoes.

Avoiding Chaos and Theft

Be thorough in your preparation and setup so you are not scrambling (trying to set up, price items, and organize them) while bargaining and selling to customers.

Never leave your sale unattended; this makes it too easy for people to grab and run. This applies also to leaving areas within your sale unattended, especially if your items cover a large area. Hint: delegate one or two people to handle sales at specified areas, e.g., lawn & garden items, clothing. This eliminates customer confusion and also frees you up to handle the cash-out area.

Have plenty of change before opening your sale. Keep lots of quarters, ones, and fives in particular.

Take money and cash-out your customers near the exit of the sale, not in the back of your garage. This will minimize the temptation for people to walk away from your sale with un-purchased items.

Keep your money on your person!! Fanny packs are great for this purpose. The worst place to keep cash is in your pockets. Do NOT place a cash box on a table. Money can easily be stolen if you are called away from your table or distracted.

Place jewelry and collectible items on the table you are using as your base. Your base should preferably be the place where you tally up a sale and make change.

Remember, the first three hours of your sale will be the busiest. If at all possible, have helpers!

Disposing of Leftovers

If you want to make money on what didn't sell, you can take pictures of the items and list them on Craigslist or on one of many other free websites available. If you prefer to donate them, there are many charities who will gladly come to your home and pick them up. Some charities also have drop off locations.

PART TWO:
HOW TO SHOP GARAGE & YARD SALES

9 THINGS TO CONSIDER WHEN SHOPPING

You may be thinking, what is there to consider? I'll just jump in my car and go! But if you really want to succeed at finding what you're looking for quickly and at a great price, continue reading!

You will want to consider:

-Weather conditions

-Type of vehicle you'll want to use or to which you have access

-Type of currency

-How to find what you're looking for

-Doing your homework on item values

-How to save gas getting to sales

-When to arrive

-Children accompanying you

-Verifying the condition of what you're buying

-How to make an offer

The next several chapters will give you tips and recommendations for all of the above considerations.

10 PREPARATION

Weather

What time of year are you attending sales? Remember that you'll typically head out first thing in the morning when there may be a chill in the air, but will warm up later in the day. Pretend you're going hiking and dress in layers. If there's a possibility of rain or snow, take gloves, a hat, or an umbrella with you.

What vehicle you have (or can rent/borrow)

This really depends on what you're looking for. If you know you'll be looking for large furniture, appliances, bicycles, or other bulky items, take a truck, SUV, or at least have one of these at your disposal. If you don't have a truck or SUV of your own, line up a friend or relative to be available. You can always pay for the item and pick it up later. Of course, you have to trust that the people won't sell it out from under you.

Currency

I cannot stress enough the importance of having small bills on your person and the benefits of using cash for your purchases. Many people hosting garage sales do not think about making change. More than once I've been caught in a situation where I'll want to buy $5 worth of items and all I have is a $20. The host can't make change so I've left empty-handed. In addition, do not take $50 or $100 bills; instead, take $20s, $10s, $5s and $1s. Many hosts are reluctant to accept $50s or $100s due to the risk of counterfeit bills. If you plan on writing a check, make sure you have a valid ID with the address on the ID matching the address on the check. Some hosts will not accept checks at all. If this is the case, you can put down a small deposit and have the person hold your item for a specified period of time while you go to the bank or ATM to get the cash.

In my experience, I have also come to realize that if you make an offer with cash in hand, hosts are more likely to make a deal with you. If you're holding a checkbook, it's as if you have enough money to pay full price!

How to find what you're looking for

MAKE A LIST SO YOU KNOW WHAT YOU'RE LOOKING FOR! My husband, children, and friends will often tell me to keep my eye out for something for them. I'll add those to my list so when I go out to sales, I can keep everyone's wishes in mind.

I personally use online sale sites, such as Craigslist and our local newspaper, to identify which sales will have items I'd be interested in. Craigslist is nice because you can go to the "Garage Sales" pull-down under "For Sale" and enter what specific town/towns are close to you. You will see the special importance of doing this as you begin mapping out your sale route.

Also, sometimes people will include a phone number on their sale ad. If they do, you can call to get further detail on items you're interested in, or maybe even get an opportunity to preview the items and to buy them prior to the sale.

Doing your homework on item values

Doing shopping homework is important so you don't overpay for items or pass up a great deal.

Use your list. Go out to online sale sites such as Craigslist or eBay and surf the specific for sale category relevant to what you're looking for (i.e., Furniture, Electronics, Baby Gear, etc.). Look at the average price people are asking for the items you are interested in and make note of this average price on your list. Now lower this price by 10%. This is be the MAXIMUM price you should pay for the item. eBay is also a great resource. Go to the web site and type in the description of your item of interest. It will show you listings of similar items for sale. On the lower left hand side, select "Completed Listings". This will give you the prices that items actually sold for. Most sellers on websites are willing to barter a bit and take less than their listing price. When I go out to sales, I typically offer 20% or 30% less than the average price on the web. More times than not, my offer has been accepted.

11 MAPPING AND SALE ETIQUETTE

Mapping

How to save gas getting to sales: use maps!

Make a list of the sales that are of interest to you including *address, start time and* what *items* they have that are of interest to you. Use a web-based tool or map and determine where exactly the sale is. Then number the sales in the shortest chronological route. Your starting point for the route may not be close to your house, BUT it could also be the first sale that you want to go to, based on the items they will be selling. If you really want to have the opportunity to buy an item of interest before anyone else, get to that sale first!

Etiquette

When to arrive

I know, it's tempting to show up an hour early and get the first pick of items as people are setting up, but this is

RUDE! Showing up 15 minutes early is usually considered acceptable, but do so only if it appears that your hosts are ready.

Children accompanying you

If you take children to sales with you, there are several things to keep in mind:

Do NOT leave young children unattended by an ADULT in your vehicle – EVER!!! It is illegal and in just a few minutes horrific things can happen – car-jackings, kidnappings, car accidents, children playing with locks, windows, doors, matches, lighters--you name it! Just don't do this.

Keep your children no further than your arm's length while shopping sales. Do not put them with the toys and expect them to stay there. They are your responsibility. If you can, go to the toys first, let them pick out an item for purchase, and then go with the children to look at the items you're interested in. This way your children will have something in their hands to keep them occupied while you shop.

If a child breaks an item at a sale you will be expected to buy it. Hence the reason it's good to put something of interest to your children in their hands so they don't break other items.

Do not let your children run around at sales. They could fall and hurt themselves, run into other patrons and hurt them, or even get hit by a car. As previously mentioned, keep them at arm's length.

Carry a bottle of hand sanitizer in your vehicle. After your children have handled items at a sale, always make sure they sanitize their hands (you should too!). This minimizes the contraction of viruses through handling items after potentially infected people have handled them.

12 INSPECTING THE GOODS

Verifying the condition of what you're buying.

Listed below are tips on making sure you get what you pay for:

Electronics

ALWAYS plug them in and make sure they are fully functional before you buy! If no power is available at the sale, do NOT buy the item.

CDs, DVDs, or Video Games – take discs out of case and inspect in the light for scratches or nicks.

Battery Operated Items

If batteries seem to dead, ask the person at the sale if they have some batteries you could use to test it with. Once you verify that the item works, return the batteries to the owner. Consider keeping a small pack of AA and AAA batteries in your car in case there are none available at the sale. They will not deteriorate in heat or explode.

Furniture and Decorative Items

Mechanically, make sure all hinges, doors, wheels, handles, etc., function properly. Aesthetically, look for cracks, chips, stress fractures, evidence of temporary repair like glue, tacks, nails, rips, tears, and wear. When purchasing upholstered furniture and bedding, be aware of the cleanliness of the people or home from whom you are purchasing the item. You don't want to take home anything that may have bed bugs, lice, mice, weevils, or any other undesirable infestation.

Toys, Bicycles, Scooters, *etc.*

Check for mechanical functionality and safety–wheel operation, brakes, handles, doors, hinges, springs, and overall construction. Only buy items that you can clean and sanitize. You will want to clean all toys purchased for your children before they play with them.

Clothing

Inspect for rips, tears, missing buttons, broken zippers and stains. Check along all seams for wear and tears. As mentioned previously with upholstered furniture and bedding, be aware of the cleanliness of the people or home from whom you are purchasing the item. You don't want to take home anything that may have bed bugs, lice, mice, weevils or any other undesirable infestation.

Miscellaneous

If you are interested in items that need assembly, ask the host how it goes together. Even if you don't fully assemble it you can make sure all of the pieces are there. If you don't go to these lengths, you may take home a tent that is missing poles, or a shelving unit missing a shelf.

Food & Personal Care Items

Unless it looks like the host is a distributor of some type, I don't recommend buying these types of items. If the host does appear to be a distributor, then look at the expiration dates and ensure that the packaging has not been tampered with. NEVER buy medications or alcohol at sales!!!

13 MAKING OFFERS

Don't feel nervous or embarrassed about offering less than the asking price. Most hosts have priced their items knowing that people will probably offer to buy the items for less. These are some suggestions when making offers:

If you're working off your list that I referenced in the previous section, "How To Find What You're Looking For", and if you did your research and noted average web prices:

Offer 20% to 30% less than their asking price for items priced $20 or more.

Offer 40% - 50% less than their asking price for items priced $10 or less.

Quick way to calculate the percentage of an item:

10% of $10 Just multiply **1x1** (10%) = $1 off

15% of $10 Just multiply 1.50x1 (15%) = $1.50 off

20% of $10 Just multiply **2x1** (20%) = $2.00 off

Hosts will probably counteroffer, going lower, somewhere between what they were asking and what you offered.

Hosts will be less likely to accept a lower price early in their sale. They may decline your offer and hope to sell it to another patron at a higher price. You can try to counteroffer again if you really want to purchase the item, or if you can pay full price.

The more you buy, the more the host is going to be willing to make you a "deal". For example, if you're buying a whole room of furniture and it totals $500 you can ask if they'll take $350. They may counteroffer at $400 because they want to get rid of it. If you're buying 20 clothing items with a total asking price of $50, offer $25 and they'll probably counteroffer you at $30. Either way, you come out ahead and they're moving many more items out of their sale.

New Unopened or Tagged Items

Hosts will try to get as close to the original purchase or replacement price as possible, so expect asking prices to be 80%-90% of retail. On these items you should only offer 10%-20% less than their asking price.

If an item is labeled "Price is FIRM", then it probably is firm, unless it is at the end of their sale and they're getting ready to close.

CLOSING NOTE

I hope this garage sale guide has been helpful to all you fellow bargain hunters out there. The information about hosting and attending either garage sales, estate sales, or community fundraisers has been gathered (sometimes painfully!) over my many years of doing all of the above. But I learned that when you have properly prepared yourself, you can have a great deal of fun. And I haven't even mentioned how much I have learned about the people who sell or buy the many fascinating items available in these venues.

Hosting and attending sales of all types has been a passion of mine for more than thirty years. I moved from New York to Colorado in 1979 with my parents. There were no garage sales, estate sales, or community fundraisers in New York, hard as that may be to believe. But Colorado was so different.

Every spring and summer weekend, my mother and I had our noses buried in the local paper, looking for amazing bargains at garage sales. We used to pore over the ads and prioritize the ones we wanted to attend, depending on what we were looking for. Then we got out the city map and developed a chronological list of addresses. The next morning, bright and early, we were off, eager to find those treasures at a bargain price. My dad would be so excited when we showed up, sometimes with a full back seat and trunk, and listen to us as we told him how we spent our day. I have such wonderful memories of those times.

Since then I have furnished and decorated several homes, clothed not only my own children, but many of my friends' children as well. I have showered those I love with gifts purchased from garage, estate, and fundraiser sales. I have hosted many successful and profitable sales and provided assistance or advice to others who wanted to know what to sell, how to advertise and stage, and how to price their items.

Last, but not least, selling and purchasing used items is also very "green". Items that are recycled through multiple hands until they are no longer useful do not fill up our landfills as quickly. In the past, accepting hand-me-downs, or buying used items, used to be thought of as a sign of poverty. Today, this is viewed as being ecologically responsible. How our times have changed! And isn't it wonderful that our thinking has changed accordingly!

That being said, keep this guide with you as you begin your weekend with the newspaper or the Internet.

Happy Sale-ing!